Faith to the Faithless

Finding Grace in Doubt and Uncertainty

Aisha A. Dennis

This is a work of non-fiction. Names, character, places and incidents either are the product of the author's experiences or are used fictitiously. Any resemblance to actual persons, living or dead, events, or locales is entirely coincidental.

Designed and published by

Leads Publishers
07075763015

Faith to the Faithless: *finding Grace in Doubt and Uncertainty*

When we are faithless,
He remains faithful."
– 2 Timothy 2:13

In a world where faith is heralded as the cornerstone of a meaningful life, many struggle with doubts, questions, and a sense of inadequacy in their spiritual journey. The pressure to exhibit unwavering belief can leave some feeling marginalized, especially when life's challenges overshadow our capacity to trust the unseen fully. Yet, as we journey through the Scriptures, we encounter a remarkable truth: God's grace is not limited to those with strong faith. It extends even to the faithless, the doubting, and those whose belief is frail.

This book, "Faith to the Faithless: finding Grace in Doubt and Uncertainty," is born out of a deep desire to explore the paradoxical nature of divine grace. It is an invitation to delve into the lives of biblical characters who still receive God's favor, healing, and blessings despite their weak or nonexistent faith. Through their stories, we uncover a powerful message that reassures us that God’s love and mercy are not confined to the strength of our faith; instead, they are displayed amid our doubts, fears, and uncertainties.

As we journey together through the pages of this book, we will explore the stories of the man at the Pool of Bethesda, the centurion's servant, the demoniac of Gadara, and other biblical figures whose faith was either weak, misplaced, or absent altogether. We will also revisit the Old Testament accounts of Naaman the Syrian, Gideon, and the Israelites in the wilderness—each narrative shedding light on how God's grace operates beyond the boundaries of human belief.

This book is not just a retelling of ancient stories; it reflects the relevance of these narratives in our contemporary lives. In today's fast-paced, often skeptical world, many wrestle with the same doubts and fears as these biblical characters. The questions they faced are the same ones we grapple with today: What happens when our faith falters? Can we still find purpose, hope, and meaning when we struggle to believe?

"Faith to the Faithless" does not aim to answer all our questions; instead, its goal is to encourage those who feel their faith is too weak to be of any value. It is a book for those who have experienced the weight of doubt, the burden of skepticism, and the challenge of maintaining faith in a world that often demands tangible evidence before individuals can believe. Through biblical examples and contemporary applications presented in these chapters, I hope to convey a message of hope: that even when our faith is small, God's grace is vast and encompassing.

Whether you are firm in your faith, someone who questions the very concept of belief, or someone who finds themselves somewhere in between, this book is for you. It is a reminder that God's grace is available to all, regardless of the strength of our faith. It is an invitation to trust in a God who sees beyond our doubts and extends His love and favor even to the faithless.

May this book serve as a source of comfort, encouragement, and inspiration as you navigate your faith journey—wherever you may find yourself on that path.

With grace and hope,

Aisha A. Dennis

August 2024

Acknowledgments

God is the author of this book and my inspiration, so I give him all the glory. I also profoundly thank my loving husband, Dr. Royal James Dennis. Your unwavering support, wisdom, and encouragement have been my strength throughout this journey. You have been my anchor, reminding me of God's grace in all things, and for that, I am grateful. And thanks to our loving children for their patience and love.

To Rev Cheryle Hanna, my mentor, and mother in the Lord, I am so thankful for your mentorship and belief in the importance of this message. You saw what others could not see in me, gave me a chance, and pushed me to pursue my call. Your wisdom and friendship have made me obedient to God's plan. Dr. Thelma Majela, my sister from another mother, thank you for your invaluable guidance, encouragement, and insight.

To Rachelle Robertson, your encouragement and steadfast support have been instrumental in my walk. You constantly reminded me of how much God has placed in me. Thank you for walking alongside me during this process and continually reminding me of the power of faith and grace.

Finally, to everyone struggling with "nonexistent faith,"—this book is for you. May it remind you that God's grace knows no bounds and that even in moments of doubt or struggle, His love and favor are ever-present.

Contact with us via

Info.hayahministries@gmail.com

Linkedlin.com/in/aish4real

instagram@aishy4real

Table of Contents

Chapter 1.

Introduction

Introduction to the concept of non-existence faith—what it is and how does it manifest.

> *"Faith is taking the first step even when you don't see the whole staircase." – Martin Luther King Jr*

According to the Bible is there such a thing as weak faith, little faith, or no faith at all? This question came to mind after I heard a young woman share the difficult story of her cousin who was told she struggles with mental health due to a lack of faith. Let's call her Mary for privacy's sake; Mary struggles with mental health challenges, so she decided to reach out to her spiritual leader in her faith community for support. Instead of offering help, the leader dismissed her struggles, telling her that her faith was weak. Well, we may not blame the spiritual leader. There could be two alternatives to his answer - he may be uneducated and unaware of mental health struggles and support, or his answer is based on the traditional belief about mental health. Thousands of spiritual leaders respond to their congregants in this manner, this may not be intentional but may be due to a lack of mental health education. This raises an important question: What does it mean to have weak faith? To explore this, we need to define faith from secular and Christian perspectives.

Faith is often depicted as a powerful, unwavering force that anchors us through life's storms. It is the assurance of things hoped for, and the conviction of things not seen—a profound trust in the promises of God. Looking at the four elements (Belief, Action, Hope, and Trust) that connect to faith, we can tell that they all depend on each other for proper functionality.

The faith diagram visually represents "Faith" at its core, glowing with a sense of warmth and light to emphasize its vital importance. Arrows connect these elements, showing their interdependence and how each strengthens the other. The four interconnected elements highlight the multifaceted nature of faith:

1. **Belief** - Illustrated with a cloud and an upward arrow, symbolizing trust in unseen or divine forces, with a hint of spiritual wisdom.
2. **Hope** - Depicted as a sunrise, suggesting new beginnings and the anticipation of a brighter future.

3. **Action** - Shown as footsteps, signifying the movement and steps one takes when acting in faith.
4. **Trust** - Visualized with an open hand, portraying reliability and the security found in faith.

Encircling the diagram are vines or branches, representing growth, and illustrating how faith helps nurture and develop personal and spiritual life. The overall feel is dynamic and life-giving, reflecting the power of faith in action. And yet, for many, faith is not always so steadfast. Instead, it can be fragile, hesitant, and riddled with doubt. This is what some Christians refer to as "weak faith." Weak faith is not the absence of belief but rather a belief that is frail, wavering, or incomplete, sometimes due to life circumstances. It exists on the spectrum between firm conviction and outright disbelief. This could result when there is a disconnect from one or more of the elements from the faith diagram. Those usually tagged with weak faith may struggle to fully trust in God's promises, often finding themselves caught between belief and doubt especially in difficult situations. This type of faith is characterized by an internal conflict where the heart yearns to believe, but the mind is plagued by uncertainties. Here is how someone's faith may waver in several ways:

- **Doubt and Uncertainty:** A person with weak faith may frequently question their beliefs or the reliability of God's promises. They may wonder if God is truly present or if He will act in their favor. This doubt can lead to a lack of confidence in prayer, worship, and spiritual practices.
- **Fear and Anxiety:** Without a solid foundation of faith, fear and anxiety often take root. The uncertainties of life become overwhelming, and the individual may struggle to find peace or hope amid trials. Fear of the future, of suffering, or God's judgment can overshadow their faith.
- **Reliance on Tangible Evidence:** Weak faith often seeks reassurance through tangible signs or evidence. This person may find it difficult to trust in what is unseen, preferring to rely on what they can see/facts, touch, or understand logically. When such evidence is lacking, their faith wavers.

- **Inconsistent Spiritual Practices:** Those with weak faith may experience inconsistency in their spiritual lives. They might pray, read Scripture, or attend worship sporadically, driven more by routine or obligation than by a deep-seated belief. Their connection to God feels tenuous, leading to a spiritual life that is often marked by highs and lows.
- **Spiritual Fatigue:** Weak faith can lead to a sense of spiritual exhaustion. The constant battle between belief and doubt can drain a person's energy and enthusiasm for spiritual growth. They may feel tired of trying to hold on to faith, leading to a gradual disengagement from spiritual practices.

How Does Weak Faith Manifest in the Bible?

The Bible presents numerous examples of individuals whose faith was weak or had no faith at all, yet who still found themselves recipients of God's mercy, healing, and favor. These stories serve as a testament to the fact that weak faith does not disqualify us from experiencing God's grace.

For instance, consider the man at the Pool of Bethesda (John 5:1-15). Similarly, the centurion sought healing for his servant (Matthew 8:5-13). In the Old Testament, Naaman the Syrian (2 Kings 5:1-14) and many more. These stories highlight how blessings can be bestowed upon those with little or no faith through the intercession of others.

The Relevance of Weak Faith Today

In contemporary life, the challenges of weak faith are as relevant as ever. In a world that often prioritizes evidence and tangible results, the struggle to maintain a strong, unwavering belief in the unseen can be daunting. Many find themselves wrestling with doubts, fears, and uncertainties, questioning whether their faith is enough to sustain them.

In secular terms, faith can often be equated with hope. People frequently express this when they say, “I’m hoping for…” But what does hope mean to us individually? According to the Oxford Dictionary, hope is "the desire and search for a future good, difficult but not impossible to attain." The key takeaway here is that the future might seem challenging, but it is not beyond reach. In the secular mindset, people believe they can achieve anything through their strength and effort. John Maxwell, in his book “The 21 Irrefutable Laws of Leadership: Follow Them and People Will Follow You, discusses how leaders must inspire hope to energize those they lead. He famously says,

> *“Where there is no hope in the future, there is no power in the present.”*

This quote underscores the essential role that hope plays in empowering us to act and live effectively in the present. When people have a vision or hope for a better future, it fuels their motivation, determination, and strength to face current challenges.

Similarly in Man's Search for Meaning, Viktor Frankl also explores the significance of hope.

He writes,

> *"Those who have a 'why' to live, can bear with almost any 'how."*

Frankl’s experience in a concentration camp taught him that having a sense of purpose and hope for the future can give individuals the strength to endure even the most difficult circumstances. But in today’s generation, how many people have a sense of purpose to continue living? People tend to succumb easily to the challenges of life. And for those who stand tall to face their trials, where does their motivation come from, given that the future is unseen? Even when God reveals aspects of the future through dreams and visions, as in the biblical examples of Joseph, Jacob, Daniel, and Samuel to mention but a few, He only shows in part. The book of First Corinthians clearly states it like this:

Now our knowledge is partial and incomplete, and even the gift of prophecy reveals only part of the whole picture! Joseph, for instance, dreamt of greatness but had no idea that he would be sold by his brothers before the dream of greatness would eventually become a reality (Genesis 37:1-36).

Maxwell's focus on the importance of a forward-looking vision as a source of strength resonates with the Christian teachings of faith and hope. In Christian belief, faith and hope are closely connected. Hebrews 11:1 state,

> *"Now faith is the substance of things hoped for, the evidence of things not seen."*

This verse shows that faith is the assurance or confidence in what we hope for, which empowers us in the present even though we cannot yet see the outcome. It is by the same faith that we accept/agree the world was created by the word of God; faith is a confidence based not on visible evidence, but on God's promises through his words. Romans 15:13 also highlights the connection between hope and power:

> "*May the God of hope fill you with all joy and peace as you trust in him, so that you may overflow with hope by the power of the Holy Spirit.*"

Here, hope is presented as something that comes from faith in God, which in turn empowers believers with joy and peace.

For believers in Christ, faith is about trusting in God's promises and waiting for those promises to be fulfilled. But what about those who do not share this belief? How does the concept of faith speak to someone who does not have Christ? And why do some people receive God's blessings while others continue to wait? Is this disparity due to weak or lack of faith as believed by some, or does it suggest that God chooses whom He wishes to bless and at his own time? This question will be explored in late chapters. For now, we will consider faith outside Christ.

Faith Outside Christian Belief:

Outside of Christianity, faith can be understood more broadly as trust or confidence in something or someone. In many religions and belief systems, faith is not only in a deity but also in the principles, moral codes, or philosophies that guide a person's life. For example:

- **Islam:** Faith (Iman) in Islam involves belief in the oneness of God, the prophets, and the day of judgment; this is what guides a Muslim's life and actions.
- **Buddhism:** Faith (Saddha) in Buddhism is more about trust in the Buddha's teachings and confidence in the path of practice, rather than belief in a deity.
- **Secular Faith:** Even in secular contexts, faith can refer to a belief in the potential for human goodness, trust in scientific progress, or confidence in one's abilities and values.

In all these contexts, faith provides a foundation that motivates and sustains individuals, helping them navigate the challenges of the present by looking forward to a future outcome.

In summary, Faith, whether understood from a secular or Christian perspective, is a powerful force that drives people to face the challenges of the present with hope for the future. In the secular world, faith often takes the form of hope and confidence in one's abilities. In Christianity, faith is intertwined with hope, rooted in the assurance of God's promises. Whether in a secular or religious context, the strength of one's faith or hope is essential for living a purposeful and empowered life.

Biblical stories of people without faith remind us that God's grace is not limited by the strength of our belief. Rather His love and favor reach out to us even in our moments of doubt and fear. Whether we are battling personal struggles, facing overwhelming circumstances, or simply finding it hard to trust in God's plan, the examples in Scripture offer us hope. They teach us that God's mercy is abundant and that He is patient with our frailties. Through the lives of biblical characters and their encounters with divine grace, we will learn that even when our faith is small, God's love for us is immeasurably great.

The Paradox of Receiving God's Favor Despite Little to No Faith

One of the most profound and intriguing aspects of the Bible is the paradoxical nature of God's favor—how it often extends to those who exhibit little to no faith. At first glance, it seems counterintuitive. After all, faith is frequently highlighted as a critical element in the relationship between God and humanity. As Hebrews 11:6 declares,

> *"And without faith, it is impossible to please God."*

Yet, repeatedly, we see instances in the bible where God's grace and blessings are bestowed upon individuals who display minimal to no faith at all. This contradiction challenges the common belief that faith is the primary prerequisite for divine intervention. Let us consider the case of the man at the Pool of Bethesda, he did not demonstrate any faith in Jesus' ability to heal him; his hope was solely in the waters of the pool. Despite this, Jesus chose to heal him, how can we explain this act of mercy? The man of Gadara, possessed by demons, was in no position to exercise faith, yet Jesus delivered him. Even in the Old Testament, Naaman the Syrian initially scoffed at the idea of washing in the Jordan River to be healed of leprosy. Naaman's obedience came more from desperation than faith, but he was still healed. These stories reveal a profound truth about the nature of God's grace and mercy:

His Grace is not bound by the strength of human faith.

God's mercy often operates independently of our belief [as seen in Centurion's Servant, Mat 8:5-13], reaching out to those who are weak, doubting, or even unaware of their need for Him. This paradox highlights the generosity and unconditional love of God, who blesses not because of our worthiness or the strength of our faith, but because of His abundant love and boundless grace.

For believers, this paradox can be both comforting and challenging. However, it reassures us that God's love is not earned nor are His blessings contingent upon our spiritual strength. God's kind of love is a decision, an action, and it is sacrificial. And Roman scripture backs it up by saying,

> *"But God showed his great love for us by sending Christ to die for us*

while we were still sinners {Roms 5:8},"

Agape love is sacrificial, it is a kind of love that is not concerned with self, but it concerns itself with the wellbeing of others. This is why God can show Favour to even those who do not acknowledge His existence.

But at the same time, it challenges the notion that only the faithful are deserving of God's favor, urging us to reconsider our attitudes toward those who struggle with belief or the unsaved. This prompts us to reconsider Apostle Paul's statement in the book of Ephesians which states that we cannot do anything to earn God's love, once we are saved, it is by grace, and not by our works.

"For it is by grace you have been saved, through faith – and this is not from yourselves, it is the gift of God– 9 *not by works so that no one can boast* {Eph 2:8-9}.

How does the unsaved perceive the above scripture without feeling neglected? The truth according to God's word- God's love still extends to the unsaved or anyone without faith; this paradox offers hope. God extended his love from the Jewish people to the Gentiles as seen in Acts 10, Cornelius and his household became the first Gentiles to inherit God love. This suggests that divine grace is available even to those who are uncertain, skeptical, or distant from God. It opens the door to the possibility that God's love and intervention are not exclusively reserved for the spiritually elite but are accessible to all, regardless of the state of their faith.

The Purpose of Exploring Weak/Non-existence Faith and Its Implications for Believers and Non-Believers Alike

In today's world, the concept of weak faith carries significant weight, particularly as many grapple with personal doubts, societal pressures, and the stigma often attached to spiritual struggles. For those within the Christian community, as well as those outside it, the exploration of weak faith reveals much about the complexities of belief and the grace of God. The exploration of weak faith is not merely an academic exercise; it has profound implications for both believers and non-believers. In contemporary society, where certainty and confidence are often celebrated, admitting to weak faith can feel like a personal failure or a sign of spiritual inadequacy. This can lead to a profound sense of isolation, as individuals fear judgment or rejection from their faith communities. The stigma associated with doubting or struggling in one's faith can be overwhelming, causing many to suppress their uncertainties rather than seek support and understanding.

For those within the Christian faith, understanding weak faith allows for a deeper comprehension of God's nature and His relationship with humanity. It provides insights into how God's grace operates beyond human limitations and challenges the often-rigid perceptions of what it means to be "faithful."

For believers, exploring wavering faith serves several key purposes:

1. Encouragement in Times of Doubt: By acknowledging that even the faithful experience periods of doubt and weakness, believers can find comfort and reassurance in scriptures like Psalms 46:1

   > *"God is our refuge and strength, always ready to help in times of trouble."*

   Stories of biblical figures with wavering faith remind us that God's love and favor are not withdrawn during these times but are often most evident.

2. Growth in Compassion: Understanding wavering faith fosters a spirit of compassion toward others who struggle with belief. Scriptures like Ephesians 4:32 become our anchor "Instead, be kind to each other, tenderhearted, forgiving one another, just as God through Christ has forgiven you." It encourages believers to support one another in times of spiritual weakness rather than judging or ostracizing those who doubt.

3. Reinforcement of God's Sovereignty: Exploring weak/wavering faith underscores the sovereignty of God, who is not limited by human belief. It reminds believers that God's plans and purposes will prevail, even when our faith falters, emphasizing His ultimate control over all things.

For non-believers or those who identify with weak faith, this exploration serves as an invitation and a source of hope:

4. **Invitation to Experience God's Grace:** The accounts of individuals who received God's favor despite their weak or non-existent faith suggest that one does not need to have everything figured out to experience God's

grace. It invites non-believers to open themselves to the possibility of divine intervention in their lives, even if their faith is minimal or absent.

5. **Challenge to Preconceived Notions:** For those who view faith as a prerequisite for divine favor, the exploration of weak faith challenges this assumption. It presents the idea that God's love is not a reward for belief but a freely given gift that can reach anyone, regardless of their spiritual state.

6. Hope in Times of Uncertainty: For those who feel distant from God or unsure of their beliefs, understanding that God's favor can still be upon them offers hope. It suggests that their doubts do not disqualify them from receiving God's blessings and that they are not beyond the reach of His grace.

In summary, the purpose of exploring weak faith is to illuminate the breadth and depth of God's grace, which extends to all, regardless of the strength of their belief. It is a topic that encourages believers to be more compassionate and understanding while offering non-believers a glimpse of the hope and love available to them through a relationship with

God. By examining the paradox of weak faith and divine favor, we gain a fuller understanding of the nature of faith itself and the boundless reach of God's mercy.

Chapter 2.

The Man at the Pool of Bethesda: Healing Without Faith

How you ever try to assist someone who never asked for your help? This narrative actual reminds me of my Africa culture compared to Canada where you must ask first before rending help. As an Africa descent, I grow up with the culture of helping those in need especially sick or the elderly without asking first.

The story of the man at the Pool of Bethesda, found in John 5:1-15, is a compelling account of Jesus' healing power, help without asking and somehow contradicts statements about faith—or the lack thereof. This narrative not only highlights miraculous healing but also serves as a profound lesson on the nature of faith, hope, and divine grace.

From this narrative, we read that the pool, called Bethsaida in Aramaic was located near the Sheep Gate in Jerusalem. Bethsaida translates to a house of Grace/Mercy, where people afflicted with many diseases come to wait with the intention of receiving healing once the water is stirred by the angel.

[3] Crowds of sick people—blind, lame, or paralyzed—lay on the porches. 5 One of the men lying there had been sick for thirty-eight years. 6 When Jesus saw him and knew he had been ill for a long time, he asked him, "Would you like to get well?"

The last phrase did not say "do you want help? Instead, he spoke about getting well. According to traditional belief, the waters of the pool had healing properties, stirred periodically by an angel, and the first person to enter the water after it was stirred would be healed of their affliction. In my thought, this man would have preferred Jesus wait around until the angel stirs the water. That way, Jesus will quickly get him into it before anyone else. Remember the man at the center of this story had been afflicted for 38 years. He had spent a sizable portion of his life by this pool, waiting and hoping for a chance to be healed. His entire hope rested on the possibility of being the first to enter the waters when it was stirred, but due to his condition, he could never get there in time. When Jesus arrived at the pool, He saw the man lying there and knew that he had been in this condition for a long time. Jesus approached him and asked a straightforward question: "Do you want to get well?" (John 5:6). At first, this question seemed unnecessary. Why wouldn't someone who had been sick for nearly four decades want to be healed? However, this question probes deeper into the man's state of mind and spirit. Jesus was not only addressing his physical condition but also his spiritual and emotional state. The man's response to Jesus reveals much about his mindset. Instead of expressing faith or asking for healing, he immediately explains why he has not been healed:

> *"Sir, I have no one to help me into the pool when the water is stirred. While*

I am trying to get in, someone else goes down ahead of me" (John 5:7).

From his response, we can sense frustration, loneliness, and tiredness, he seems to be giving up mentally. Does this man's statement sound like what some contemporary Christians would call lack/weak Faith? Oh yes, it does. His response is not one of faith in Jesus or in a miraculous healing through divine power, but rather a resigned explanation of why his efforts have been in vain.

Lack of Faith in Christ

The man's hope was entirely fixated on the pool's waters, not on the person standing before him—Jesus, the Son of God, who had the power to heal with a word. He did not recognize Jesus or see Him as a source of healing. His lack of faith in Christ is evident; he did not even ask Jesus for help. His expectation was solely limited to the physical and the familiar, the pool and its supposed healing properties. Familiarity can be a double-edged sword. On one hand, it provides comfort and a sense of security, as we become accustomed to certain routines, people, or beliefs. On the other hand, familiarity can lead to complacency, where the extraordinary becomes ordinary, and the sacred becomes mundane. This is particularly dangerous when it comes to our relationship with God. **When we become too familiar with spiritual practices, religious rituals, or even the concept of God Himself, we tend to eliminate God from the equation—turning our faith into mere routine without the reverence and dependence that true worship requires.** The Bible warns against complacency and self-reliance.

Proverbs 1:32-33 exhorts us to,

> *"For the turning away of the simple will slay them, And the complacency of fools will destroy them, But whoever listens to me will dwell safely,*
>
> *And will be secure, without fear of evil. (NKJV]"*

This scripture highlights the importance of keeping God at the center of our lives, relying on Him rather than our familiar routines or understanding. The story of this man highlights a significant aspect of his life: his faith was not in Christ but in a ritualistic belief surrounding the pool. He was so focused on the tangible, on what he had known for years, that he could not see beyond it to recognize the true source of healing standing before him. This story can resonate with many believers and Christian leaders. When we become accustomed to what we know and what works, we resist change and throw caution to the new move of God and His divine power.

Jesus' Act of Healing

Despite the man's lack of faith, Jesus, in His compassion and authority, simply said to him, "Get up! Pick up your mat and walk" (John 5:8). Immediately, the man was cured; he picked up his mat and walked. This miraculous healing did not depend on the man's faith or belief in Jesus—it was an act of divine grace and power.

Jesus' command and the man's subsequent healing underscore the theme that God's grace is not always contingent on human faith. The man did not have to believe in Jesus' ability to heal him for the miracle to occur. This challenges the conventional understanding that faith is always a prerequisite for receiving God's blessings. In this case, the man's healing was a demonstration of God's sovereign will and mercy.

The Aftermath and Revelation

After the healing, the man was confronted by the Jewish leaders because he was carrying his mat on the Sabbath, which was considered work and, therefore a violation of the Sabbath law. When questioned, the man did not even know who had healed him, as Jesus had slipped away into the crowd. It is safe to say the man was unsaved. Later, Jesus found the man at the temple and said to him,

"See, you are well again. Stop sinning or something worse may happen to you" (John 5:14).

This encounter suggests that Jesus was concerned not only with the man's physical well-being but also with his spiritual state. The call to stop sinning indicates that Jesus' healing was an invitation to a deeper, transformative faith, one that goes beyond physical healing to encompass spiritual renewal.

The story of the man at the Pool of Bethesda is a powerful illustration of God's grace operating independently of human faith. Despite the man's focus on the pool and his lack of recognition of Jesus, he received healing. This narrative challenges the idea that faith is always a necessary condition for receiving God's favor. It also invites readers to reflect on where they place their hope—whether in the familiar and tangible or in the person of Jesus Christ, who offers true healing and transformation. For believers, this story is a reminder that God's grace can reach us even when our faith is weak or misplaced. For non-believers or those struggling with doubt, it offers hope that divine favor is not beyond their reach, even if they have not yet come to faith. The man's healing at the Pool of Bethesda therefore serves as both a miracle of physical restoration and a profound lesson in the unexpected ways God's grace can manifest in our lives.

Divine Mercy Beyond Faith: Jesus' Decision to Heal Despite the Man's Misplaced Hope

The story of the man at the Pool of Bethesda, as narrated in John 5:1-15, is a profound example of divine mercy that transcends human faith. The man's healing by Jesus, despite his misplaced hope in the pool's waters rather than in Christ, highlights the nature of God's grace—unmerited, unconditional, and often bestowed regardless of the recipient's level of faith or understanding.

- ***The Man's Misplaced Hope***

The story of the man at the Pool of Bethesda is a profound example of divine mercy that transcends human faith. The man's healing by Jesus, despite his misplaced hope in the pool's waters rather than in Christ, highlights the nature of God's grace—unmerited, unconditional, and often bestowed regardless of the recipient's level of faith or understanding. For 38 long years, the man at the Pool of Bethesda had suffered, caught in a cycle of pain and despair. His hope for healing was anchored in the widespread belief that the pool's waters possessed miraculous powers. He was convinced that if he could just be the first to step into the water when it was stirred, he would be healed. However, his physical limitations always prevented him from reaching the water in time. As a result, his hope remained fixated on a physical remedy that consistently let him down.

- **Jesus' Act of Divine Mercy and the Nature of Divine Mercy**

Despite the man's lack of faith in Jesus and his misplaced hope in the pool, Jesus, in an act of divine mercy, chose to heal him. Jesus simply said, "Get up! Pick up your mat and walk" (John 5:8). Immediately, the man was healed—his physical condition was restored, and he was able to walk. This act of healing is a striking example of mercy that goes beyond the conventional understanding of faith as a prerequisite for receiving God's favor. The man did not ask Jesus for healing, nor did he express any belief in Jesus' ability to heal him. Yet, Jesus healed him anyway. This underscores the truth that God's mercy is not always dependent on human faith or understanding. God's grace can reach us even when our faith is weak, misdirected, or absent.

Divine mercy, as demonstrated by Jesus in this narrative, is a powerful force that operates beyond human limitations. It is not constrained by our level of belief, our understanding, or our actions. God's mercy is freely given, often in ways that defy our expectations or understanding.

This story illustrates that God's actions are not always a response to human faith but are often an expression of His sovereign will and compassion. Jesus saw the man's need, his long years of suffering, and his hopeless situation, and responded with mercy, even though the man did not recognize or ask for it. This emphasizes the idea that God's love and mercy are proactive, reaching out to us even when we are not reaching out to Him.

- ***Contemporary Implications***

In contemporary life, this narrative invites us to reflect on how we perceive God's mercy and how we understand faith. It challenges the notion that we must have perfect or strong faith to receive God's blessings. Instead, it reassures us that God's mercy is available to all, regardless of the strength or direction of their faith.

For those who struggle with doubt, who feel that their faith is too weak or misplaced to warrant God's attention, this story is a profound reminder that God's mercy is not limited by human frailty. It offers hope to those who feel unworthy or distant from God, affirming that His grace can reach them even in their moments of uncertainty or misunderstanding.

For believers, it is a call to trust in the boundless nature of God's mercy and to extend that same grace to others. It encourages a compassionate approach to those whose faith may be weak or wavering, recognizing that God's mercy is at work in ways that we may not fully understand.

The healing of the man at the Pool of Bethesda is a testament to the depth and breadth of divine mercy, which transcends human faith. Jesus' decision to heal, despite the man's misplaced hope, illustrates that God's mercy is not earned but given freely, often in unexpected ways. This story reassures us that even when our faith falters or is misdirected, God's grace remains available to us, offering healing, hope, and restoration.

Contemporary Application: Misplaced Focus and Undeserved Grace

In today's world, many people find themselves, like the man at the Pool of Bethesda, placing their hope in solutions that ultimately fail to deliver what they need. Whether it is relying on material wealth, personal achievements, or even certain rituals and practices, people often turn to these sources with the expectation that they will bring fulfillment, healing, or purpose. Yet, just as the man's hope in the pool's waters was repeatedly disappointed, so too are many of these modern pursuits unable to meet the deeper needs of the human heart.

- ***Focusing on the Wrong Solutions***

People today might focus on career success, social status, or even self-help philosophies as the keys to overcoming life's challenges. They might believe that if they work hard enough, achieve enough, or follow the right steps, they can fix their problems and find happiness. However, like the man's reliance on the pool, these solutions often fall short. They may provide temporary relief or satisfaction, but they do not address the deeper, spiritual needs that only God can fulfill.

Despite this, many find themselves recipients of God's grace even when their focus is on the wrong solutions. Just as Jesus extended mercy to the man at the pool despite his misplaced hope, God often intervenes in our lives with grace and blessings, even when we are looking in the wrong direction. This demonstrates that God's love and mercy are not contingent on our perfect understanding or strong faith.

- ***God's Intervention in Weak or Misdirected Faith***

God's intervention in our lives, even when our faith is weak or misdirected, underscores the nature of His grace. It is not something we earn through perfect faith or right actions, but something God freely gives out of His love and compassion. This is a profound comfort for those who struggle with doubt or feel their faith is insufficient. It shows that God's mercy can reach us regardless of where we place our hope or how strong our faith is.

In contemporary life, this means that even when we are focused on the wrong things—whether it is material success, relationships, Addictions, or self-reliance—God's grace is still available to us. He can intervene in our lives in ways we do not expect, bringing healing, guidance, and blessings, often when we least deserve it. This encourages us to shift our focus from self-reliance to reliance on God, recognizing that His grace is the true source of our strength and hope.

The relevance of God's intervention, despite our weak or misdirected faith, is a powerful reminder of His boundless mercy. It shows us that even when we are focused on the wrong solutions, God's grace can still break through, offering us the healing and hope we truly need. In a world where it is easy to place our trust in things that fail us, this truth encourages us to turn our focus back to God, knowing that His mercy is always available, even when our faith is not where it should be.

Chapter 3.

The Centurion's Servant: The Power of Proxy Faith

Biblical Narrative: The Roman Centurion and His Servant (Matthew 8:5-13)

The Story of the Roman Centurion

Have you cared about the needs or problems of others? To the point that you start looking for solutions such as rendering prayers in secret/open, calling to support or even just being there? In Matthew 8:5-13, we encounter the story of a Roman centurion, a man of authority and power, who approached Jesus with an urgent request. His servant, whom he valued highly, was lying at home paralyzed, suffering terribly. Despite being a Gentile and a figure of authority in the Roman Empire, the centurion displayed remarkable humility and faith. He did not consider himself worthy to have Jesus come under his roof, but he believed in Jesus' authority to heal from a distance. He said to Jesus:

> *"But just say the word, and my servant will be healed" (Matthew 8:8).*

Jesus marveled at the centurion's faith, declaring that he had not found anyone in Israel with such great faith. As a result of this faith, Jesus granted his request, and the servant received instant healing. As we can see from this narrative, the servant was not even aware his master was seeking a solution to his illness; in other words, the servant had no faith, and yet his master's faith got him healing

> *Then Jesus said to the centurion, "Go! Let it be done just as you believed it*

> *would." And his servant was healed at that moment [NIV]."*

One striking aspect of this narrative is the passive role of the servant in the healing miracle. There is no indication that the servant was aware of the centurion's request or that he had any faith of his own in Jesus' ability to heal him. The servant's healing was entirely initiated by the centurion's faith and concern for his beloved servant. The focus is on the centurion's interaction with Jesus, his expression of faith, and Jesus' response to that faith. The servant, who is the direct recipient of the miracle, remains in the background, his faith or awareness of the miracle unmentioned. This aspect of the story highlights an important biblical theme that God's mercy and power can extend to individuals regardless of their faith or involvement. The servant benefited from the centurion's faith without any action on his part, illustrating that God's grace can reach people even when they are passive or unaware.

Like the centurion's servant, the paralytic man's healing is initiated by the faith of others—in this case, his friends (Mark 2:1-12). There is no mention of the paralytic man's faith or request for healing; instead, it is the active, visible faith of his friends that moves Jesus to act.

> *When Jesus saw their faith, he said to the paralyzed man, "Son, your sins are forgiven [Mark 2:5, NIV]."*

This parallels the centurion's situation, where it was the centurion's faith, rather than the servant's, that led to the healing.

Both stories highlight the power of intercessory faith—the idea that the faith of one person can bring about divine intervention on behalf of another. These narratives underscore the significance of communal faith and prayer, showing that God can respond to the faith of others to bring healing and blessing to those who might not be in a position to ask or believe for themselves. This underscores the empowering role of faith in our lives, giving us hope and assurance in God's intervention.

Faith of the Centurion

The story of the centurion in Matthew 8:5-13 highlights the extraordinary faith of a Roman military officer who sought Jesus to heal his servant. Despite being a Gentile and an outsider to the Jewish faith, the centurion demonstrated a profound belief in Jesus' authority and power. He understood that Jesus did not need to be physically present to heal his servant; instead, the centurion confidently declared that just a word from Jesus would be enough: "But say the word and my servant will be healed" (Matthew 8:8).

Jesus marveled at the centurion's faith, noting that he had not found such great faith even among Israel. The centurion's faith was remarkable because it reflected not only his deep trust in Jesus' divine power but also his humility. He acknowledged that he was unworthy of Jesus to come under his roof yet fully believed in the authority Jesus carried. This expression of faith brought about the immediate healing of his servant.

The centurion's faith was not just intellectual acknowledgment but a living, active belief that God could intervene in his servant's dire situation. His faith serves as a model of trust in God's power to act, even without direct, physical contact or visible evidence. The faith he exhibited became the channel through which divine healing flowed, underscoring that God's power responds to faith, regardless of one's background or status

Comparison to Today's Belief

In today's context, this story challenges common assumptions about faith and healing. It challenges the assumption that healing is contingent on the individual's faith. In both the centurion's and the paralytic's stories (Mark 2:1-12), the recipients of healing did not express personal faith, yet they received divine intervention because of the faith of others on their behalf. This narrative, however, suggests that God's mercy can transcend individual faith, reaching even those who may not actively seek it or express belief. The servant's passive role serves as a reminder that God's grace is not limited to those who actively demonstrate faith; it can also be extended through the faith of others. This has significant implications for how we understand prayer and intercession in contemporary life. Intercessory faith is just as relevant today. Many people might be in situations where they are unable to believe for themselves—whether due to illness, despair, doubt, or ignorance of God's power. The prayers and faith of others can act as a bridge to God's healing and intervention. Just as the centurion believed for his servant and the friends of the paralytic man believed for their friend, we, too, can bring others before God through our faith and prayers, trusting that He will act on their behalf.

Furthermore, this story underscores the inclusive nature of God's grace. The centurion, a Gentile and outsider to the Jewish faith, received a powerful affirmation from Jesus because of his faith. This breaks down barriers and challenges the notion that God's blessings are reserved for a select few. It reminds us that God's grace is available to all, regardless of background, status, or personal faith. This inclusivity of God's grace makes us all feel accepted and valued in His eyes.

Modern Parallels

In modern life, we frequently see parallels where the faith and prayers of loved ones lead to divine intervention. A common example is when family members pray for someone who is sick or going through a challenging time, and despite the sick person's lack of faith or even awareness, they experience healing or breakthrough. Many testimonies of miraculous healings involve people being lifted by the faith of their church, friends, or family members who consistently pray for them.

During the Middlebelt Great Awakening conference 2024 in Africa, my husband visited the hospital to pray for a young boy who has been sick for a long time. While praying for this boy, an elder man with a terminal disease in the same room received his healing instantly and was discharged the next day. This elder man has been terminally ill, and the doctors has pronounced a death sentence after trying all they could. The testimony was that as my husband prayed for the boy, the elderly man's daughter believed that her father would receive healing, and he was indeed healed. The next day, the family called to testify of God's goodness. The family members ended up volunteering during the conference as an appreciation to what God did in their family. This is just one testimony, there are countless stories of people who were seriously ill or in life-threatening conditions, but through the persistent prayers of loved ones, they experienced sudden recoveries or improvements that doctors could not explain. These modern parallels mirror the biblical accounts, illustrating how God honors intercessory faith. It also demonstrates the communal aspect of faith, where believers support and lift one another in prayer, trusting God to act even when the person in need is unable to express faith themselves.

In conclusion, the faith of the centurion underscores a key spiritual principle: faith need not be directly held by the person receiving the blessing for God to act. This principle continues to apply today, where the faith and prayers of one person can lead to healing, deliverance, or blessings for another. Intercessory faith is a powerful force in the life of believers, reminding us that through our prayers, we can stand in the gap for others and bring them before God, trusting in His divine intervention. Whether in biblical times or contemporary life, God's response to faith remains unwavering and transformative

Chapter 4.

The Man of Gadara: Deliverance Without Request

The Biblical Narrative (Mark 5:1-20)

Again, Jesus helping someone without asking if they needed the help. As I read this narrative, I cannot stop thinking about how Jesus' compassion would have landed him into trouble or even Jail in the Canadian society. People would call it "invading their privacy" yet all he was trying to do was help. The narrative account of the man of Gadara, as recorded in Mark 5:1-20, is one of the most dramatic accounts of Jesus' power over evil and compassion. Jesus and His disciples crossed the Sea of Galilee, a significant body of water in the region, and arrived in the region of the Gerasenes, a place known for its Gentile population and its association with the Roman military. It was here that they encountered a man possessed by a multitude of demons. This man, often called the demoniac of Gadara, lived among the tombs, isolated from society. He was in a critical state—physically, mentally, and spiritually tormented by the demonic forces within him. The demoniac's condition was so severe that he was uncontrollable. He would break the chains and shackles used to bind him, roaming among the tombs and mountains, crying out, and cutting himself with stones. His situation was one of utter hopelessness; he could not seek help or deliverance on his own, as the demons had complete control over his mind.

There was a shift when Jesus arrived; the demons immediately recognized Him and, through the man, cried out,

"What do you want with me, Jesus, Son of the Most High God? In God's name do not torture me!" (Mark 5:7).

The demons knew they were powerless before Jesus and begged Him not to send them out of the region but instead into a herd of pigs nearby. Jesus granted their request, and when the demons entered the pigs, the entire herd rushed down the steep bank into the sea and drowned. After the demons left, the once-tormented man was found sitting, clothed, and in his right mind, fully restored. The transformation was so profound, so dramatic, that the people of the region, who had previously feared the man, were now afraid of the power that had healed him. Despite their fear, the man wanted to follow Jesus, but Jesus told him to go home to his family and tell them how much the Lord had done for him and how He had shown him mercy. What a dramatic turnaround for someone who was too insane for faith business.

The Man's Lack of Faith

A remarkable aspect of this narrative is the complete lack of faith or ability to seek Jesus on the part of the demoniac. Unlike other healing stories where individuals approached Jesus in faith, this man was incapacitated by his condition. The demons within him recognized Jesus and spoke through him, but the man himself was not in a position to express faith or even seek out Jesus for help. His condition reflects an extreme form of spiritual and physical bondage, where the individual is so oppressed that he cannot act on his own behalf. His encounter with Jesus was not initiated by him but by Jesus' decision to cross into the region and confront the forces of evil. This highlights the depth of Jesus' compassion and authority; He sought out and delivered a man who was completely helpless, unable to even ask for help due to the overwhelming control of the demons.

Contemporary Relevance

The story of the demoniac of Gadara has deep relevance in contemporary discussions about spiritual bondage, mental illness, and the power of divine intervention. It illustrates that Jesus' mercy and power can reach even those who are so lost that they cannot seek help for themselves. In today's context, this might be compared to individuals who are trapped in situations of addiction, mental health crisis, or other forms of deep despair, where they feel powerless to change their circumstances. Much like the demoniac, people today may find themselves in situations where they cannot muster the faith or strength to seek God on their own. This narrative provides hope that God's grace can still reach them. It reassures us that Jesus is willing and able to intervene, even when we are at our lowest point and cannot reach out to Him. It also challenges believers to intercede and pray for those who are in such situations, trusting that God can work in their lives even when they seem beyond help

Jesus' Compassionate Deliverance

In the story of the demoniac of Gadara, Jesus' compassionate nature is powerfully demonstrated. This story parallels the widow's Son at Nain in the gospel of Luke 7:11-17. The widow did not ask Jesus to bring her son back to life, however, out of compassion He did anyway. We can see the same pattern here, despite the complete inability of the Gadarene to express faith or seek help, Jesus chose to intervene and deliver him from the demons that had tormented him for years. The man's hopeless condition, living among tombs and cut off from society, did not deter Jesus from showing mercy. Jesus did not require a display of faith or even a request for healing; instead, He took the initiative to confront the demonic forces and free the man. This shows that Jesus' compassion reaches beyond human ability or effort, extending to those who are unable to ask for help due to the depth of their suffering. Jesus' deliverance of the demoniac illustrates that divine mercy is not dependent on an individual's faith or strength. It reflects God's heart for those who are marginalized, broken, or lost, demonstrating that His grace can break through even the most hopeless situations. The man's transformation from being controlled by demons to sitting calmly, fully restored—emphasizes Jesus' power and willingness to intervene in even the darkest circumstances.

Contemporary Application

This narrative has profound relevance in addressing severe personal challenges that many face today, such as mental illness, addiction, and other forms of deep despair. Much like the demoniac of Gadara, individuals struggling with these issues often feel powerless, unable to reach out for help, or even recognize the possibility of healing. In such situations, their capacity for faith might be diminished or non-existent, making it difficult for them to seek God or express belief in recovery.

However, the story of Jesus' intervention in the life of the demoniac offers hope. It suggests that divine intervention is not limited to those who can actively believe or pray for it. God can work in the lives of individuals who are incapacitated by their struggles, whether through mental health challenges, substance abuse, or any other overwhelming condition. His grace can reach into the most inconvenient situations and bring about healing, even when a person cannot express faith themselves. This concept also highlights the importance of intercession and community support. Just as Jesus took the initiative to heal the demoniac, loved ones and communities, including his family, played a crucial role in his healing journey through prayer and support, trusting that God will intervene even when an individual cannot ask for help. It reminds us that no one is beyond God's reach, and that healing and transformation can occur in ways that defy human limitations, offering hope to those who may feel lost or abandoned in their suffering.

The story of Jesus healing the demoniac of Gadara provides a profound reminder of God's boundless mercy and power to deliver, even when a person lacks the capacity for faith. In today's world, as we grapple with severe personal challenges like mental illness and addiction, this story offers hope that divine intervention can occur even when an individual cannot actively seek it.

This narrative reminds us that God's power is not limited by our circumstances or capacity to believe. It also calls us to be compassionate towards those who are trapped in situations where they cannot help themselves, trusting that Jesus can bring healing and restoration, just as He did for the demoniac. Jesus' compassionate deliverance shows that no one is beyond God's reach, and His grace can transform even the most hopeless situations.

Chapter 5.

Naaman the Syrian: Healing Amidst Skepticism

Biblical Narrative (2 Kings 5:1-14)

Naaman was a high-ranking Syrian military commander respected by his king, the King of Aram. Naaman was known to be successful in his battles. However, he suffered from leprosy, a debilitating skin disease that brought physical suffering and social isolation. His status as a leader could not protect him from this affliction. This story began when a young Israelite girl, who had been captured in war and is now a servant to Naaman's wife, tells her mistress that a prophet in

Samaria (Elisha) could heal Naaman. This unexpected source of guidance plays a crucial role in Naaman's healing journey. Upon hearing this, Naaman goes to the king of Syria, who sends him with a letter to the king of Israel, expecting a diplomatic solution. The letter reads:

> *"With this letter, I am sending my servant Naaman to you so that you may cure him of his leprosy (verse 5, NIV)."*

However, the king of Israel, distressed by the request, recognizes that he does not have the power to heal leprosy. The Bible says he tore his robes!

> *As soon as the king of Israel read the letter, he tore his robes and said, "Am I God? Can I kill and bring back to life? Why does this fellow send someone to me to be cured of his leprosy? See how he is trying to pick a quarrel with me! (Verse 7, NIV)."*

The king quickly recognized his limitation; he knew that the supernature must exchange hands in this situation. Otherwise, war may break out between Israel and Syria. But when Elisha hears of the problem, he sends word to the king, inviting Naaman to come to him for healing. Naaman, expecting a grand display, is initially offended when Elisha sends a messenger instructing him to wash seven times in the Jordan River to be healed.

Naaman's Initial Skepticism

Naaman's reaction reveals his skepticism and his reliance on worldly expectations. He was indignant because he had anticipated a dramatic healing process fitting his status. He may have expected the prophet to personally come out, wave his hand, and invoke God elaborately. His pride, sense of superiority, and reliance on earthly methods clouded his ability to trust in a simple, faith-based solution. This initial skepticism is a common struggle, one that many of us can relate to in our own spiritual journeys.

Naaman's initial reliance on worldly methods is reflected in the following:

- **Expecting a personal audience with Elisha**: His high status made him think he deserved a special ritual, not a message sent through a servant.

- **Questioning the simplicity of the Jordan River**: He argued that the rivers of Damascus (Abana and Pharpar) were superior to the Jordan, demonstrating a lack of understanding of God's power working through simple means.

Skepticism is common among those who rely on human wisdom or pride instead of trusting God. Naaman's mindset mirrors how people often expect God to work in ways that align with their logic, status, or sense of worthiness.

Faith in Action: The Turning Point

Despite Naaman's initial refusal, his servants, showing great wisdom and humility, convinced him to obey the prophet's instruction. They reasoned with him, pointing out that if Elisha had asked him to do something difficult, he would have done it—so why not do something so simple? Their argument was a turning point for Naaman. His willingness to listen to others, let go of his pride, and act in obedience marked his shift from skepticism to faith. This turning point in Naaman's journey is a powerful reminder of the transformative power of faith and obedience.

"Now I know that there is no God in all the earth, except in Israel" (2 Kings 5:15).

Spiritual Implications of Naaman's Healing

Naaman's healing offers deep spiritual insights:

- **Faith in God's methods over human reasoning**: Naaman learned that God's ways often defy human expectations. Elisha's simple instruction symbolized the power of faith and obedience over worldly logic and status.
- **Humility as a pathway to healing**: Naaman's healing was only possible after he humbled himself, listened to his servants, and trusted God's simple command. This emphasis on humility underscores its importance in spiritual growth. Pride and reliance on status had initially kept him from accepting the solution. **God's grace extended to outsiders**: Naaman was a Gentile, yet God healed him, demonstrating His grace and mercy are available to all who come to Him in faith.

This healing foreshadows the universal nature of God's salvation, reaching beyond the boundaries of Israel.

Parallels to Contemporary Life

Naaman's story is relevant today in how people often seek complex or worldly solutions to their problems, missing the power of simple faith and obedience. It speaks to those who may be skeptical of faith-based approaches to healing—whether physical, emotional, or spiritual—and encourages a shift from reliance on worldly methods to trust in God's wisdom. It also reminds us that God's power is not limited by status, nationality, or personal qualifications; His healing and grace are available to all who humble themselves before Him. The implications of Naaman's healing for the contemporary reader are profound, offering insights into the power of faith, the importance of humility, and the universal nature of God's grace.

God's Patience and Grace

Elisha's Role in Guiding Naaman Toward Healing Despite His Weak Faith

Elisha played a pivotal role in Naaman's healing, acting as God's representative and guiding Naaman despite his skepticism and fragile faith. Here's how Elisha demonstrated patience and grace in this situation:

- **Silent Confidence**: Elisha did not meet Naaman in person but sent a messenger with the simple instruction to wash in the Jordan River seven times. This move can be seen as a test of Naaman's willingness to humble himself and trust in God. Elisha understood that healing would be physical and spiritual, requiring Naaman to surrender his pride and embrace faith.
- **Non-Confrontational Approach**: Elisha's indirect handling of Naaman's healing was an act of grace. Rather than confronting Naaman's doubts directly or berating him for his pride, he allowed Naaman to work through his resistance. Elisha let Naaman's

internal transformation unfold naturally, trusting God's timing.

- **Patience in the Process**: Naaman initially stormed off in anger, but Elisha's message still lingered. It was through Naaman's own servants, who gently urged him to reconsider, that he finally chose to obey. This reflects how God's patience is sometimes mediated through others around us and how faith can develop gradually. Elisha remained steadfast in his instructions and trusted that Naaman would come around.

Elisha's role embodies God's grace, showing that faith must not be perfect at the outset for God to work. Elisha knew that God could heal Naaman despite his weak faith. Through patience and allowing Naaman to take small steps of obedience, the prophet led him toward both physical healing and a deeper spiritual realization

- *Contemporary Application*

Trusting God's Methods Even When They Seem Too Simple or Unconventional: Naaman's initial reaction to Elisha's instruction resonates with many people's hesitation toward God's methods when they seem too simple or out of step with worldly logic. Sometimes, people expect elaborate solutions for their problems through success in their careers, relationships, or personal healing. But God often uses humble and insignificant methods to accomplish profound results.

- **God's Wisdom in Simplicity**: The Jordan River was a simple, unimpressive setting for such a miraculous healing. In the same way, God often works through humble circumstances to display His power. This principle is seen throughout the Bible, whether David, a shepherd boy, defeating Goliath or Jesus healing people through simple commands like "*Go in peace*" or "*Take up your bed and walk.*" It challenges us to trust in the simplicity of prayer, faith, and obedience, even when worldly logic calls for something grander.

- **Releasing Control**: Trusting God requires letting go of personal expectations and releasing the need to control outcomes. This is especially difficult in today's culture, which values self-reliance, and complicated solutions. However, Naaman's story encourages believers to trust in the simplicity of God's promises and the power of obedience, even when they do not fully understand the process.

- ***Modern Examples of Individuals Who Find Healing or Success Despite Initial Doubt***

- **Corrie Ten Boom**: A Dutch Christian who, during World War II, initially doubted God's plan after her family was imprisoned for hiding Jews from the Nazis. In her book *The Hiding Place*, she shares how her faith was tested in the face of suffering and death. Despite her doubts, she later found emotional healing and purpose, becoming an advocate for forgiveness and reconciliation. Her journey from doubt to faith mirrors Naaman's experience, where God's grace worked despite initial skepticism.
- **C.S. Lewis**: A well-known author and theologian, Lewis began as a skeptic, declaring himself an atheist in his early life. Yet, through a gradual process of self-reflection and the influence of Christian friends, he came to faith

in God. His book *Surprised by Joy* captures his journey from doubt to belief, illustrating how God's grace can work through intellectual resistance. Despite his initial doubts, Lewis became one of the most influential Christian apologists of the 20th century.

- **Contemporary Examples of Addiction Recovery**: Many people who enter recovery programs initially doubt that something as simple as attending meetings or following a 12-step program could help them overcome life-threatening addictions. Yet countless stories show individuals finding healing and freedom from addiction by trusting the process, even when it does not make sense to them. The act of surrendering to a higher power, as emphasized in many recovery programs, mirrors Naaman's eventual humility and obedience, leading to miraculous transformation.

In conclusion, Naaman's healing is a powerful reminder that God's grace and patience extend even to those with doubts or weak faith. Elisha's role in the story highlights how God uses others to guide us, and how faith can grow through small acts of obedience. The lesson of trusting God's methods, even when they seem too simple or unconventional, is as relevant today as it was in ancient times. The simple act of obedience, rooted in humility, becomes a conduit for God's miraculous power.

Chapter 6.

Gideon's Hesitation: Victory Despite Doubt

Biblical Narrative (Judges 6:36-40)

In Judges 6:36-40, Gideon, a chosen judge of Israel, repeatedly asks God for confirmation that He will save Israel through him, despite receiving clear instructions. This is demonstrated in the famous "fleece test," where Gideon asks God to make a fleece wet with dew while the surrounding ground remains dry. When God fulfills this request, Gideon asks for the reverse to happen as a final confirmation. God grants both signs, demonstrating His patience with Gideon's uncertainty and fear.

Gideon's Hesitancy and lack of Faith

Gideon's repeated requests for signs from God reveal a man struggling with self-doubt and not so strong Faith, so to speak. Despite being called a "mighty warrior" by the angel of the Lord (Judges 6:12), Gideon does not see himself as capable of leading Israel to victory. His hesitation shows the tension between human weakness and divine promise, a struggle that many of us can relate to. Gideon's need for reassurance reflects his desire to believe, yet his lack of confidence in God's promises leads him to ask for repeated signs.

This narrative highlight God's willingness to meet Gideon in his doubts. Rather than reprimanding him, God responds graciously, providing the assurances Gideon needs to step into his role. This grace demonstrates that Faith does not always mean the absence of doubt but instead trusting God to fulfill His promises, even when our Faith is fragile.

Application

The story of Gideon encourages believers to move forward in obedience, even amid doubt and uncertainty. It reminds us that God understands human hesitation and meets His people where they are, guiding them toward victory despite their fears.

This theme can be powerful when applied to modern-day struggles, showing how God's patience and grace can lead to victory even when our Faith falters.

Divine Patience and Empowerment

God's Response to Gideon's Doubts

God's response to Gideon's doubts is a profound example of divine patience. Rather than becoming frustrated with Gideon's repeated requests for signs, God meets him with understanding and compassion. Gideon's doubt, expressed through the "fleece test" (Judges 6:36-40), represents a deep insecurity in the face of a daunting task. But rather than condemning him, God accommodates Gideon's need for assurance. When God called Moses to deliver Israel, he gave excuses [Exo 6:12] and asked for signs that

God gave through Aaron [Exo 7]. God's willingness to provide multiple signs demonstrates His long-suffering nature. This patience highlights a key aspect of God's character: He knows our weaknesses and insecurities and is willing to engage with us through them. Gideon's hesitation did not disqualify him from being used by God, showing that doubt does not eliminate us from God's purposes.

Empowerment of Gideon to Lead Israel

After addressing Gideon's doubts, God continues to equip him for leadership. Despite his initial fear and reluctance, Gideon is empowered to lead Israel to victory over the Midianites. This empowerment is a process that builds throughout the narrative, mirroring the gradual strengthening of our own faith as we trust in God's promises.

1. **Calling and Reassurance**: God calls Gideon a "mighty warrior" (Judges 6:12), speaking into his identity long before Gideon sees himself in that light. This sets the stage for Gideon's transformation from doubt to becoming a courageous leader.
2. **Confirmation through Signs**: The signs God provides through the fleece and the earlier

sign of consuming Gideon's offering with fire (Judges 6:21) serve as repeated confirmations of God's presence. These divine interventions gradually strengthen Gideon's Faith.

- **Divine Strategy**: In Judges 7, God reduces Gideon's army to 300 men, further demonstrating that victory would not come by human strength but by God's power. This final act of reducing the army emphasizes that God is the source of empowerment, not human ability, instilling in us a sense of reliance on God's power rather than our own strength. Despite his initial fears, Gideon ultimately led Israel to a miraculous victory over the Midianites, fulfilling his calling. This victory is a powerful demonstration of God's ability to use imperfect people, like Gideon, to accomplish His purposes. It reassures us that our doubts and imperfections do not disqualify us from God's plans.

Application: God's Empowerment in Weakness

Gideon's story is a powerful reminder that God does not demand perfect Faith but rather a willingness to trust and obey. He patiently works through our doubts and insecurities, empowering us to follow His plans. Gideon's journey illustrates that divine empowerment comes not through human strength or certainty but through God's faithfulness.

In contemporary life, this story reassures us that even in our moments of doubt or weakness, God is working to strengthen and equip us for the tasks He has called us to. It invites us to trust His power, even when our own feels insufficient.

Contemporary Application

God's Patience: A Pathway to Growth in Faith

In modern life, the story of Gideon provides a profound message about God's patience and how it aids our spiritual growth. Just as Gideon experienced doubt and insecurity, we often face seasons where our faith wavers. The key takeaway from Gideon's story is that God does not abandon us in our doubt. Instead, He patiently nurtures our Faith through:

- **Repeated Assurances**: Like Gideon, we may find ourselves seeking confirmation from God about our purpose or direction. God's willingness to give Gideon signs reflects His understanding of our need for reassurance, especially when we face overwhelming challenges.

- **A Process of Growth**: Gideon did not become a mighty warrior overnight. His journey with God was one of gradual strengthening, where each step of obedience built his confidence in God's promises. This shows us that Faith is not static but a dynamic growth process. God patiently works with us, allowing room for our questions while guiding us toward deeper trust.
- **Grace for Our Weakness**: Often, we may feel that our doubts disqualify us from being used by God, but Gideon's story reveals the opposite. God's patience with our weaknesses expresses His grace, and He is more concerned with our willingness to follow Him than having perfect Faith from the outset.

Doubting Yet Chosen and Empowered for Great Tasks

One of the most relevant aspects of Gideon's story is that even in our doubts, God can still choose us for significant purposes. The relevance of this idea is profound in today's world, where uncertainty and self-doubt are everyday struggles. Key takeaways include:

- **God's Call Is not Dependent on Our Confidence**: Gideon was reluctant, hesitant, and doubtful, yet God still called him to lead Israel. This teaches us that God's calling on our lives is based on His plans, not our sense of worthiness or certainty. In a culture that often emphasizes self-confidence as a prerequisite for success, Gideon's story reminds us that God can use us even when we do not feel "ready" or "qualified."
- **Trusting in God's Strength, Not Our Own**: Gideon's success in defeating the Midianites did not come from his personal strength or ability but from God's power. This principle applies today when faced with tasks far beyond our capacity. Rather than relying solely on our skills or resources, we are invited

to lean on God's strength, knowing He equips us for what He calls us to do.

- **Faith Is not the Absence of Doubt, but Obedience Despite It**: Gideon's story shows that doubt and Faith can coexist. Gideon doubted, yet he obeyed God's command to lead the army. This encourages us to take steps of Faith even when we have questions or uncertainties. Faith in action, even in the presence of doubt, leads to growth and victory.

Encouragement for Modern Believers

For modern believers, Gideon's story offers hope and encouragement. It tells us that God understands our humanity and is patient with our hesitations. We can take comfort in knowing that our doubts do not disqualify us from being used by God. Instead, God invites us to trust Him, even when our Faith feels weak, empowering us to accomplish remarkable things through His strength, not our own.

In today's world, where many face uncertainty about their purpose or calling, Gideon's story reminds us that God's plans are greater than our fears. God is working to strengthen and equip us for the tasks He has called us to. He patiently guides us, even when we feel least capable.

Chapter 7.

The Israelites in the Wilderness: Provision Amidst Complaints

Biblical Narrative (Exodus 16:1-15)

This chapter beautifully highlights the Israelites' journey through the wilderness after their exodus from Egypt, illuminating their challenges with complaints and a wavering faith in God's provision. In Exodus 16:1-15, these newly freed Israelites face the harsh realities of the wilderness, expressing their hunger and fear of starvation as they grumble against Moses and Aaron. Despite having witnessed God's miraculous deliverance from Egypt, their faith falters, leading them to question whether God can truly provide for their needs in the desert.

The Israelites lamented to Moses and Aaron, saying, "If only the Lord had killed us back in Egypt. There, we sat around pots filled with meat and ate all the bread we wanted. But now you have brought us into this wilderness to starve us to death."

The Lack of Faith Displayed by the Israelites

Their complaints reveal a profound struggle to trust in God's goodness, even after witnessing His mighty works. This section reflects a common human tendency to doubt God's care during uncertain times, emphasizing the struggle to maintain faith in His presence and power when faced with adversity.

God's Continued Provision

In response to their complaints, God demonstrated grace rather than anger. He provided manna from heaven and quail to satiate their hunger. This part of the chapter underscores God's unconditional love and patience, showcasing that His provision hinges not on the strength of human faith but on His unwavering steadfastness. Even in the midst of their faltering faith, God's enduring care illustrates His desire to sustain and nurture His people, even when their trust wavers.

Then the Lord spoke to Moses, saying, "Look, I'm going to rain down food from heaven for you. Each day, the people can go out and gather as much food as they need for that day. I will test them in this to see whether or not they will follow my instructions."

Contemporary Application

Today, we can resonate with the struggles experienced by the Israelites. Like them, we often find ourselves grumbling and doubting in the face of challenges or uncertainties. Our faith can drift during difficult times, leading us to question God's provision when life takes unexpected turns.

How God Continues to Meet Our Needs Even When Our Faith is Faltering

As we reflect on the parallels between the Israelites' story and our own lives, we recognize how God continually provides for us, even amid doubt. His faithfulness is not reliant on our unwavering trust; it stands as a powerful testament to His grace and love. This theme reinforces the inspiring message of hope that just as God provided for the Israelites despite their complaints, He continues to meet our needs and care for us during our most uncertain moments

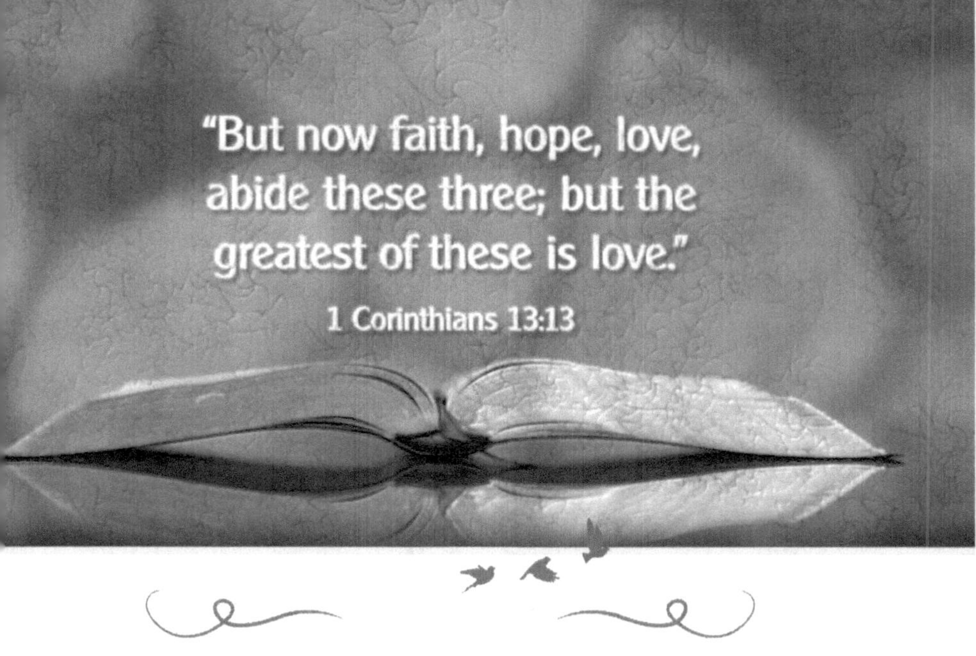

Chapter 8.

Faith, Hope, and Purpose in Contemporary Life

The Relevance of Weak Faith Today

In today's fast-paced world, weak faith manifests in numerous ways. This section explores how doubt, fear, and reliance on worldly solutions often take center stage when individuals face personal crises. Despite technological advancements and modern conveniences, people still encounter moments of deep uncertainty, where faith seems to wane under pressure. This portion could discuss the common experiences of doubt in a world that prizes logic, self-reliance, and tangible results over spiritual trust, showing how faith is often overshadowed by these modern distractions.

Finding Purpose Despite Weak Faith

Weak or wavering faith does not disqualify individuals from discovering their purpose. In this section, the narrative can offer reassurance that even in moments of spiritual weakness, individuals can still find meaning and direction. Drawing on personal stories, psychological insights, and biblical examples, this part would illustrate how one can navigate life's journey with an evolving sense of faith. Purpose is not always found in moments of certainty but can emerge from struggles, questions, and doubts. It emphasizes that purpose and meaning can coexist with weak faith, as God continues to guide even in our uncertainty.

Hope Beyond Faith

Hope often persists even when faith seems absent. This section can focus on contemporary stories of individuals who have experienced life-altering breakthroughs despite having little or no faith. It highlights how hope can serve as a guiding force, helping people to persevere even when belief falters. By sharing testimonies of those who have overcome significant challenges—whether in health, relationships, or career—without relying heavily on faith, this section emphasizes that hope can be a powerful tool in keeping people connected to the possibility of change and transformation.

The Role of Community and Intercession

Faith is not meant to be cultivated in isolation. This section will emphasize the importance of community and intercessory prayer in sustaining and strengthening faith. The support of a faith-based community can offer encouragement, wisdom, and prayers that stand in the gap for those struggling with weak faith. This part can feature stories of how communities have played a pivotal role in renewing hope, fostering belief, and bringing about miracles through intercession. It emphasizes the biblical principle of "bearing one another's burdens" and how collective faith can uplift individuals during moments of personal doubt.

[2] *"Share each other's burdens, and in this way obey the law of Christ* (Galatians 6:2)".

Together, these themes connect faith, hope, and purpose, showing how even in moments of weakness or uncertainty, God's plans and provision can still unfold through the support of others and the strength of hope.

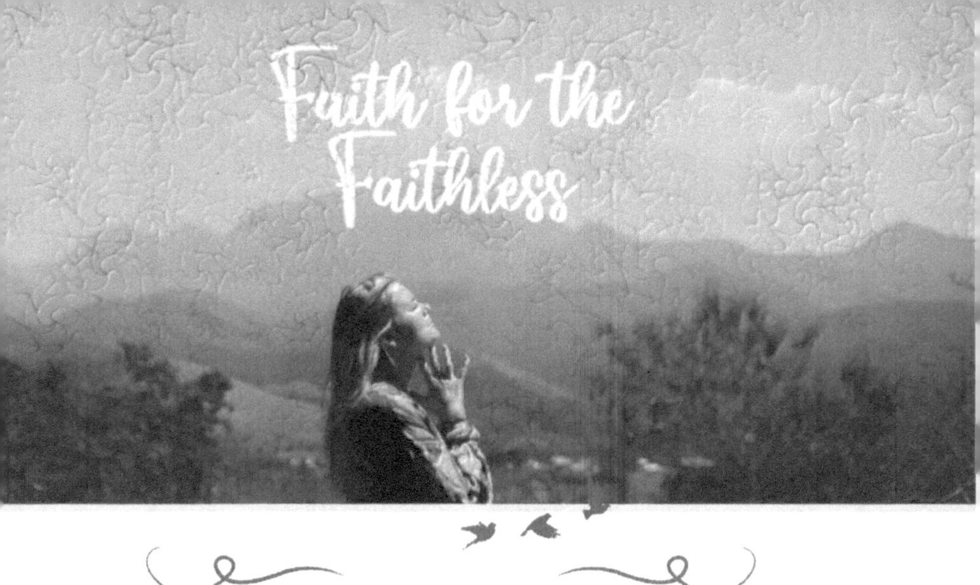

Conclusion

The Boundless Reach of God's Grace

This concluding chapter, the key biblical examples explored throughout the book are revisited to emphasize the central theme: God's grace triumphs even in the presence of weak faith. From the Israelites in the wilderness to the man at the pool of Bethesda, and the various stories of healing and provision despite doubt or disbelief, these narratives remind us that God's favor is not dependent on the strength of human faith. Instead,

God's grace flows generously, regardless of the limitations and uncertainties that individuals may face.

The Overarching Theme of God's Grace Extending Beyond Human Limitations of Faith

The central message of this chapter focuses on the idea that God's grace is boundless—it transcends human failures, doubts, and limitations. No matter how weak, wavering, or absent one's faith might be, God's grace is still at work. This part will encourage readers to let go of any pressure to have "perfect" faith in order to receive God's blessings. Instead, it emphasizes that grace is given freely and generously, not as a reward for strong faith, but as an expression of God's unending love and mercy for all people.

Encouragement for All Readers

The book closes with a word of hope and encouragement for all readers, reminding them that weak or little faith does not disqualify anyone from receiving God's grace. This section reassures readers that God meets them where they are, and His love is not conditional on their ability to maintain unshakable belief. By trusting in the limitless reach of God's grace, they can find peace, purpose, and hope, even in moments of spiritual struggle. The ultimate message is one of inclusivity and grace, affirming that everyone—regardless of their faith journey—can experience God's goodness and favor.

This chapter serves as both a conclusion and a call to action, inviting readers to embrace God's grace with open hearts, knowing that even their weakest moments are met with divine love and care.

Final Thoughts

God's grace is mysterious, boundless, and far beyond human comprehension. It often exceeds our expectations, and our understanding of what faith should look like. While we may think that only the faithful or the spiritually strong are worthy of God's blessings, the truth is that His grace reaches even the weakest, the doubting, and the faithless. His favor is not limited by our shortcomings but flows generously to all.

This book aims to guide readers through the complexities of faith—especially the struggles with weak or little faith. Through biblical examples and contemporary reflections, it demonstrates that God's grace is available to everyone, even those wrestling with doubt and fear. The stories shared in these pages show that God's intervention and blessings are not confined to those with unwavering belief but extend to those whose faith falters and to those who may not even have faith at all.

Ultimately, this book offers a message of hope, a reminder that God's grace is always at work, even in the lives of those who feel unworthy or unsure. It is a call to embrace the vastness of His love and to trust that He meets us exactly where we are, with grace that is boundless and unending.

Helpful Resources

Reflection and Counseling Tools

Faith Exploration Exercises

- Journaling prompts for readers:
    - *"When have I received grace without asking or being deserving?"*
    - *"How can I extend grace to someone who lacks faith?"*

Guided Scriptures for Reflection

- Psalm 34:18 – God is near to the brokenhearted.
- Isaiah 41:10 – Assurance of God's presence in moments of weakness.
- Romans 8:26 – The Spirit intercedes when faith is faltering

Community and Ministry Resources

- **Celebrate Recovery** – A Christian program designed to help people overcome life's hurts and habits, often including testimonies of renewal from moments of faithlessness.
- **GriefShare** – For those struggling with doubt and grief, showing how faith can be rekindled.
- **Pastoral Counseling Resources** – Tools to guide those who feel distant from God but are open to spiritual healing.

Sources

- Chick, Jonathan. "Recovery: Twelve simple steps to life beyond addiction." (2015): 103-103.
- Howard Jr, David M. "" Surprised by Joy": Joy in the Christian Life and in Christian Scholarship." *Journal of the Evangelical Theological Society* 47, no. 1 (2004): 3.
- *Henry Nouwen: The Return of the Prodigal Son* – Reflections on the parable's relevance for modern struggles with faith.
- Ten Boom, Corrie, Elizabeth Sherrill, and John Sherrill. *The hiding place*. Chosen Books, 2006.
- https://www.talktotheword.com/p/psalm-1074-7-meaning.html
- (2015). An Observation and Analysis of Ordinary Bible Reading among British,

Evangelical, Emerging Adults. https://core.ac.uk/download/30

- *Philip Yancey*: *What's So Amazing About Grace?* – A book exploring how grace impacts faith and life.
- *Tim Keller*: *The Prodigal God* – Insights on God's mercy for the faithless and estranged.

Scriptural References

New Testament

- **John 5:1-15** – *Healing at the Pool of Bethesda*
(The man didn't display faith, yet Jesus healed him out of grace and compassion.)
- **Matthew 8:5-13** – *The Healing of the Centurion's Servant*
(The faith of the centurion, not the servant, was the basis of the healing.)
- **Mark 5:1-20** – *The Demoniac in the Region of the Gadarenes*
(A man possessed by demons was healed and transformed despite his initial helplessness.)

- **Luke 7:11-17** – *The Widow's Son at Nain* (Jesus raised the widow's son without being asked, purely out of compassion.)
- **Matthew 9:18-26** – *Jairus' Daughter and the Woman with the Issue of Blood* (Faith is highlighted, but the miraculous actions of Jesus extended to those on the periphery of faith.)
- **Luke 15:11-32** – *The Parable of the Prodigal Son* (A story illustrating restoration even for those who stray from faith.)

Old Testament

- **2 Kings 5:1-14** – *Healing of Naaman* (Naaman's healing came despite his initial pride and lack of understanding of God.)
- **Jonah 1-4** – *God's Compassion on Nineveh* (A city far from faith experienced God's mercy.)
- **Exodus 16:1-35** – *Manna in the Wilderness* (God's provision to the Israelites despite their grumbling and lack of trust.)
- **Psalm 107:4-7** - Wandering in a desert wasteland

(God's compassion and deliverance for those who are lost, physically or spiritually.)

www.ingramcontent.com/pod-product-compliance
Lightning Source LLC
LaVergne TN
LVHW091113150826
845673LV00002B/809

* 9 7 9 8 2 3 0 5 3 7 2 5 0 *